ABOUT THE AUTHORS

Paul Ankers has degrees in exercise and sports science from London and Exeter Universities. As a judo competitor he competed at international level, including World Championships and two Olympics.

He now runs a sports injuries, rehabilitation and exercise clinic in Surrey. His clients include many well-known sports competitors, British sports teams and the British Olympic Association, TV, media and entertainment personalities, as well as people requiring special remedial exercise programmes and programmes following surgery or cardiac illness.

Paul Davidge is the founder and managing director of Lifestyle Engineering Ltd, a company which produces personal Lifestyle Fitness Programmes for clients around the world. He has helped Paul Ankers to develop the programme and wrote the *Sunday Times* magazine series about it. He has kept fit using body-circuits and The Lifestyle Fitness Programme for the past five years.

ACKNOWLEDGEMENTS

On behalf of Paul Ankers and myself, I would like to express my thanks to Richard Girling at the *Sunday Times* magazine for developing and editing the magazine series and giving us help and advice along the way. Thanks also to photographer Graeme Montgomery and Tony Chambers from the *Sunday Times* magazine for enduring six days of shooting pictures of wooden models, Kati Pauk for proof-reading and help with the manuscript, and Michael Stewart-Smith, my parents and Andrew Cainey without whose continued support this book would not have been possible.

Further thanks for the photographs and illustrations go to Penny Sobr and Allan Drummond (illustrations), Gary Cochran (wooden hand), Windsor & Newton, Lucienne Roberts and Jane Harper (wooden models), and Conran Design (wooden chair).

Paul Davidge, July 1991.

DISCLAIMER

Although this programme has been designed to be as safe as possible, neither the publisher nor the authors can accept any responsibility for any injury or illness suffered whilst following the Lifestyle Fitness Programme or any other form of exercise. You should seek medical advice before you undertake any fast, vigorous or competitive sport or exercise without gradually developing an adequate level of physical fitness, particularly if you are over the age of thirty-five. Similarly, if you have had any form of heart disease or stroke, if you have any physical injuries or disabilities that influence your ability to exercise, or if you are in any doubt about your health or ability to exercise, you should seek specialist advice before you start. Most importantly, if during exercise or after, you feel ill, unwell, or any pain (especially in the chest), you must not exercise further but see your GP, doctor or specialist exercise adviser.

THE SUNDAY TIMES
LIFESTYLE
FITNESS
PROGRAMME

PAUL ANKERS

WITH

PAUL DAVIDGE

A Pan Original
PAN BOOKS
LONDON, SYDNEY AND AUCKLAND

First published 1992 by Pan Books Ltd
Cavaye Place, London SW10 9PG

9 8 7 6 5 4 3 2 1

© Paul Ankers and Paul Davidge 1992

ISBN 0 330 32515 9

Photoset by Parker Typesetting Service, Leicester
Printed in England by Clays Ltd, St Ives plc

C O N T E N T S

THE CORONARY PREVENTION GROUP

For most of human history, from the Stone Age onwards, daily life has been physically demanding. Until a little over a hundred years ago, back-breaking agricultural or manual work occupied most people. But today, with technology advancing at an accelerating pace, many of our daily work routines involve nothing more physically strenuous than standing or sitting for long periods and for some people the car has all but replaced their legs.

Unfortunately, we inhabit the modern world with what are still, basically, Stone Age bodies. There is now an impressive array of scientific evidence which shows that without some kind of regular physical work or exercise, our bodies become prey to a whole range of physical and mental ailments.

Take coronary heart disease, for example. For forty years or more, survey after survey from all over the world has shown that physically active people are less likely to have coronary heart disease or to die from it than sedentary folk. As recently as 1990, the published results of a ten-year study of almost 10,000 male civil servants showed that those who reported being vigorously active at least twice a week had less than half the heart attacks of the other men. Or, to look at it another way, being inactive can double your risk of coronary heart disease.

Given what is now known about the effects of exercise on the heart and various physiological systems, the result of this study is not at all surprising. Physical activity exercises the heart muscle itself and increases the efficiency of the lungs. This means that with each breath and beat of the heart, more blood, carrying more oxygen, is pumped through the body. At rest, the heart can beat more slowly and during exertion the heart can meet extra demands without undue strain.

Exercise has also been shown to have a beneficial effect on a number of risk factors associated with coronary heart disease. The level of cholesterol in the blood, for example, may fall and, although the reduction is not great, it is the artery-clogging type of cholesterol – low density lipoprotein (LDL) – which falls the most, leaving a higher proportion of benevolent high density lipoprotein (HDL) cholesterol circulating in the blood.

Scientists are now turning their attention to the potential clot-busting effects of exercise. The indications are that it is something in the acute phase of coronary heart disease – when a clot forms and blocks a narrowed artery – that is affected by exercise. It is not yet clear how exercise might interfere with the clotting process but in the meantime the wise course of action is to exercise your body.

In the process, your body will lose fat, which is itself a risk factor for coronary heart disease, is linked to some cancers and is a known hindrance to the control of other medical problems such as arthritis. Losing fat by exercising is not the same as losing weight, since fat will be replaced by muscle which is heavier than fat. So the scales may show a loss of two kilos of weight which may actually represent four kilos of fat loss.

Gaining muscle is also an advantage since it can help improve posture and prevent one of the most common and painful complaints: back trouble. The other main advantage of replacing fat with muscle is enhanced body tone and definition – in other words, less flab.

This alone might account for the reduced depression and better self-image claimed by many exercisers. Careful studies have also shown that exercise can lower blood pressure, reduce stress and promote regular, restful sleeping patterns. Other studies have reported improved mental alertness and an overall feeling of well-being amongst regular exercisers. This may be due in part to the fact that exercise encourages the release of endorphins, hormones which can create a feeling of euphoria in some people.

Is there no end to the benefits of exercise? Perhaps not. In fact women can add yet another advantage to the already lengthy list. Exercise can help prevent osteoporosis, the weakening of the bones which accelerates after menopause and the condition which is responsible for many of the debilitating bone fractures suffered by elderly women in this country.

In short, there are no known ill effects to regular physical activity provided that it is undertaken sensibly and safely. The rules for safe exercise are simplicity itself: start gently, build up slowly, and if it hurts – stop! Most exercise injuries and, even more rarely, deaths are caused not by exercise but by ignoring these simple rules. Remember the Stone Age body. It is designed for movement, but not meant to be shaken violently, bounced repeatedly on a hard surface or made to shift immense weight over and over again.

The Coronary Prevention Group supports the use of technology, and other instruments of change, to encourage rather than discourage physical activity. Building swimming pools, leisure centres and sports complexes is one aspect of this approach. Creating cleaner, safer city centres for people to walk and cycle in is another. Better public access to the sports facilities in educational institutions would also help, as would the provision of amenities at factories, offices and shops.

Home exercise programmes, such as the Lifestyle Fitness Programme, have an important role to play, because they are effective, convenient and easy to slot into the modern lifestyle.

Finally, remember that exercise is not miraculous. It will not save us from the ill effects of smoking or a diet stuffed with fat, salt and sugar. However, it will almost certainly improve the quality of life, without having to abandon all the labour-saving technologies on which we have come to depend.

Jeanette Longfield
THE CORONARY PREVENTION GROUP

INTRODUCTION

Dear Reader,

Thank you for buying the Lifestyle Fitness Programme, the exciting new work-out that is tailor-made to work for *you*. Thousands of satisfied customers around the world follow the Lifestyle Fitness Programme for four main reasons:

o   It is tailor-made to *your* existing level of fitness and *personal to you*.

o   It is short, taking only twenty minutes per day, three times per week.

o   It gives quick results. You will see the difference in just a few weeks.

o   It gives you an all-round fitness benefit, improving your muscle tone, shape, stamina and aerobic fitness.

HOW IS IT PERSONAL TO ME?

No two bodies are the same, so no standard exercise programme can work equally well for everyone. That is why, before you start to exercise, we ask you to spend a few minutes testing your current level of fitness so that you can work out a programme that is just the right level for you. We give you all the information you need to match your current level of fitness to a graded series of body-type exercises and put together a personal programme.

As your fitness level improves, you choose whether you want to change your exercises or increase the number of repetitions to make your programme harder. It is up to you.

HOW MUCH TIME WILL IT TAKE?

It takes only twenty minutes, three times a week! With ever-increasing demands on our time, this is essential for a fitness programme to be successful. You do not need any special equipment and can easily follow the programme at home in a small space.

WHO DEVELOPED THE LIFESTYLE FITNESS PROGRAMME?

The Lifestyle Fitness Programme is based on the work of Paul Ankers, now one of Britain's top exercise physiologists. As a judo competitor in the eighties, he competed at international level, including World Championships and two Olympics. He holds degrees in exercise and sports science from London and Exeter Universities.

He now runs a sports injuries, rehabilitation and exercise clinic in Surrey. His clients include many well-known sports competitors, British sports teams and the British Olympic Association, TV, media and entertainment personalities, as well as people requiring special remedial exercise programmes and programmes following surgery or cardiac illness. As an exercise expert, he has appeared many times on radio and TV.

The Lifestyle Fitness Programme is based on the scientific approach Paul takes when prescribing exercise for his clients, each programme tailored precisely to their individual needs. In 1991, *the Sunday Times magazine* published a seventeen-page, three-week series on the Lifestyle Fitness Programme, which in turn has led to this book.

HOW DOES IT WORK?

The programme uses body-based exercises with a large range of movement and gives you a balanced all-round fitness benefit to improve your muscle tone, shape, stamina and aerobic fitness. Using the scientific principles of exercise physiology, the exercises are arranged so that they are performed one after the other in a structure called a 'circuit' which is a safe and efficient way of exercising. The exercises are gently progressive and are suitable for men and women of all ages and abilities.

WHY EXERCISE AT ALL?

The answer may seem obvious but have you really thought about it? Different people exercise to achieve different things so your programme should take your aims into account. Work out exactly what you want to get out of *your* programme. Here are some common goals:

o Shape and tone specific, or all, parts of your body.

o Improve your general sense of well-being, skin tone and your overall appearance.

o Control your weight, by reducing the amount of fat on your body.

o Reduce your stress level and increase your energy.

o Reduce the possibility of heart and blood vessel disease, helping you live longer, more actively.

Most people say that they would like to take more exercise. Think for a moment now about exactly *why* you want to be fit.

WILL I BE ABLE TO KEEP MYSELF MOTIVATED?

By buying this book, you have taken an important first step towards getting fit but it is vital that you now exercise consistently for six weeks. After that, you will be used to exercising and the change in your body and fitness level will encourage you to continue. Here are some hints to get you through those first six weeks:

o If possible, try to get used to exercising at the same time every day, so exercise becomes part of your daily routine, whether it be just after you wake up or at the end of the day. (The only drawback to exercising late in the evening is that after raising your pulse you may find it hard to fall asleep.)

○ Aim to exercise the same number of times a week and try to stick to your target. If for some reason, you do not achieve your target during a week, do not give up or become demotivated. There is specific advice on what to do in these instances in chapter 6.

○ Try not to see exercise as a chore but as something positive you are doing for yourself. Make it as enjoyable as you can. Listen to your favourite music as you exercise, eat well and treat yourself (not with something too fattening!) as you get fitter.

○ Think about the benefits you are going to achieve – very soon!

○ If you find it hard to exercise on your own, start a pro-gramme at the same time as a friend or your partner. That way you can exercise together and motivate each other. Alternatively, supplement your programme with a weekly exercise class at your local health club or sports centre. Also, make sure you enlist the support and encouragement of your friends and family before you start.

Remember, fitness is as much a positive mental attitude as physical exercise.

WHAT DO I DO NEXT?

Turn the page and get started on your path to fitness.

Good luck!

PAUL ANKERS   PAUL DAVIDGE

ASSESSING YOUR PERSONAL FITNESS

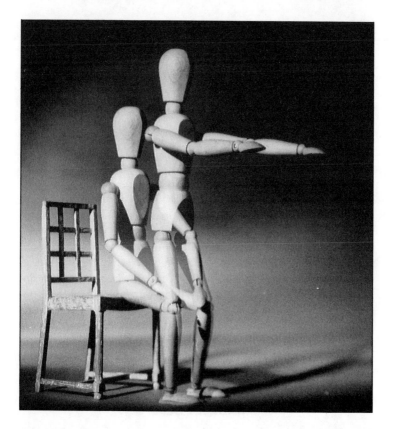

The first step is to test your current level of fitness. Your personal Lifestyle Fitness Programme will be based on your results and they will also serve as a benchmark against which you can measure your future progress. It is important that you are honest when taking these tests. You are not competing against anyone else so it does not matter how high or low your score is. The more accurate your results are, the more suited your personal programme will be to you.

Before you begin your warm-up and the exercise tests, read this section on your pulse.

YOUR PULSE

Before you start to exercise, you need to measure your resting pulse and work out the safe pulse limits within which you should exercise. If, during exercise, your pulse rate is too low, you may not be working hard enough really to benefit from the exercise. If your pulse is too high, you may be working too hard which is dangerous.

WHAT IS THE PULSE?

Your heart is a muscle about the size of your fist. See if you can clench your fist sixty times a minute. You will probably be surprised how hard it is. Yet this is what your heart does every minute of every day. Like any other muscle, the heart becomes weaker if it is not exercised, so it is important that you work it at the correct intensity during your fitness programme. You do this by monitoring your pulse. When you feel your pulse, you are feeling the surge of blood as it is pumped from your heart, pushing against and expanding the walls of your arteries.

Try both of the following pulse-taking methods to see which you prefer. Practise taking your pulse several times and soon you will find it easy.

RADIAL PULSE

The radial pulse is taken from the wrist (*see photograph*). Turn the hand palm upwards and place two fingers of the other hand lightly at the base of the thumb and wrist joint. Take your pulse with your fingers and *not* with the thumb (which has its own strong pulse and may cause double-counting).

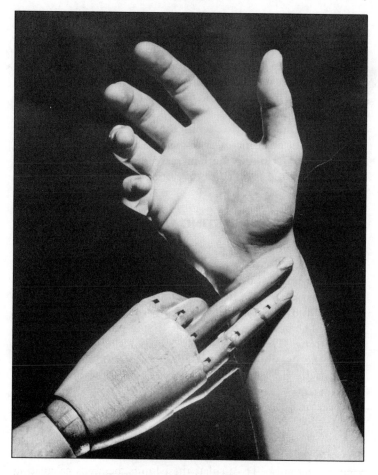

CAROTID PULSE

The carotid pulse is taken from the side of the neck (on the carotid artery), under the hinge of the jaw. Place two fingers lightly on the neck to find the beat. Take the pulse with the fingers, *not* the thumb, and do not press too hard.

Your pulse rate changes throughout your life and can even vary significantly throughout the day depending on what you are doing. Your pulse is at its lowest rate just after you wake up and rises during the day. The following are important influences:

Exercise Your pulse quickly increases with strenuous activity.
Age Your pulse increases slightly with age.
Sex Women's pulse rates tend to be five to ten beats per minute faster than men's.
Digestion Your pulse rises whilst digesting a meal.
Emotion The pulse increases with stress or nervousness.
Smoking and Drinking Both increase your pulse rate.
Stimulants Coffee and tea both stimulate the pulse.

YOUR RESTING PULSE RATE

To measure your resting pulse rate, begin by relaxing and making yourself comfortable in a sitting position (standing up raises your pulse). Locate your radial or carotid pulse and count the number of beats in fifteen seconds, *counting the first beat as 0*. Then multiply the number of beats by 4 to calculate the rate per minute. The best time to take your resting pulse is first thing in the morning. This is the lowest or 'basal' rate of the day. To reduce the possibility of error, take two counts and average them. Write the result in the two Resting Pulse boxes in the chart on page 9.

YOUR PULSE TARGETS

The safe pulse limits during exercise depend on your age and your resting pulse. To calculate these limits, begin by calculating your Pulse Range by subtracting your Resting Pulse (per minute) and your age in years from 220. For example, if you are 45 and your Resting Pulse is 70 then your Pulse Range is $220 - 45 - 70 = 105$. Write the figure in the two Pulse Range boxes below. Complete the other two boxes by writing in your Resting Pulse.

To calculate your lower pulse limit (LPL), *multiply* your Pulse Range by 0.60, then **add** your Resting Pulse.

To calculate your upper pulse limit (UPL), *multiply* your Pulse Range by 0.80, then **add** your Resting Pulse.

Example: If your pulse range is 105 and your resting pulse is 70, your lower pulse limit is found by multiplying 105 by 0.6 and adding 70. The answer is 133. Your upper limit is 105 × 0.80 + 70 = 154.

Pulse Range		Resting Pulse			
105	× 0.60 +	70	=	133	Example **LPL**
105	× 0.80 +	70	=	154	Example **UPL**
111	× 0.60 +	72	=	138.6	= **LPL**
111	× 0.80 +	72	=	160.8	= **UPL**

LPL = Lower Pulse Limit   **UPL** = Upper Pulse Limit

These are your safe pulse limits during exercise. At this level you are exercising hard enough to benefit your heart, but not so hard as to endanger your health.

You should take your pulse immediately after you stop exercising and again one minute later. Use the same method as you did when calculating your resting pulse rate. Multiply the pulse counts by 4 to work out your pulse rate in beats per minute.

The first pulse should be between the limits you have just calculated. If it is less than the lower limit, then try to perform your exercises more vigorously next time. If it is higher than the upper limit, then you *must* perform your exercises less vigorously in future. Your second pulse should be below the lower limit.

The difference between the first and the second pulse is very important. It shows the rate at which your heart is recovering after exercise and how fast it is returning to its resting state. As you get fitter, you will see that your heart recovers more quickly. The steeper the drop, the better. After 10 minutes' rest, your pulse rate should be below 100 (25 beats per 15 seconds). It will drop much faster than this if you are fitter (dropping by up to 70 beats in 1 minute if you are very fit).

Recording both of your pulse measurements each time you exercise will help to give you a good idea of your progress.

WHAT IS FITNESS ANYWAY?

There is no single measure of physical fitness. It depends upon a number of separate components. The most important of these are the *three S's* of strength, stamina and suppleness.

Strength is the force a muscle can exert and depends primarily on the size of the muscle and the number of muscle fibres that can be brought into action at any one time. Examples of daily strength activities include digging, gardening and carrying shopping or luggage. Strength sports include shot-put, tug-of-war and sprinting.

Stamina, the ability to repeat a muscular action over and over again, or to sustain a muscular contraction, depends on the functioning of the cardiovascular system (heart, blood vessels and lungs). This is the ability of the body to transport food and oxygen to the muscles efficiently, and to carry waste products away from them. Stamina is therefore closely linked to heart fitness and cardiovascular or 'aerobic' fitness. Stamina activities include climbing long flights of stairs and brisk walking. Sports include running, swimming, cycling and rowing.

Suppleness measures the range of movement in the muscles and joints. Activities include stretching up to reach shelves and DIY. Sports include dancing and gymnastics.

Improving your fitness will also have an affect on three more S's – your skill (especially your co-ordination), speed and your sex life.

Think for a moment how important each of these S's is to *you*.

WARM UP AND COOL DOWN

Before you exercise, you should *always* warm up. This raises your pulse and prepares your body to work out. Your warm up should also move your joints through their full range so you are not left stiff or sore after exercising.

Similarly, you should not stop exercising suddenly because this may result in dizziness or 'blood pooling'. Instead you

should perform gradually easier exercises to cool down and return your body to a near resting state.

Follow the instructions for six exercises below to warm up. After a while you will have memorized them. Remember to perform them every time before you exercise. By performing these exercises *in reverse order*, you can use the warm up routine as a cool down.

ARM CIRCLING FORWARDS AND BACKWARDS

Stand with your feet slightly more than hip-width apart. Start to lift your arms up in front of you, keeping your head up. Lift them past your ears (as close to the ears as possible) then turn them backwards and complete the circle

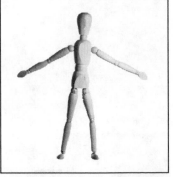

to return to the starting position. Do this 5 to 10 times. Repeat the movement with the arms going forward, so that the arms come from behind your head as close to the ears as possible, creating as large a circle as possible. Do this for 5 to 10 minutes.

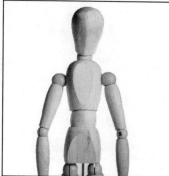

NECK ROLL

Stand upright with your feet facing forwards. Place your hands on your thighs and drop your chin to your chest. Now gently move your head over so that the left ear comes to the left shoulder then return your head to the centre with chin to chest. Next, gently move the head so that the right ear  comes to the right shoulder and return again. That counts as one repetition. Do this 5 to 10 times.

 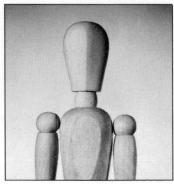

SHOULDER SHRUGS

Stand with your hands on the outsides of your thighs, feet a little more than hip-width apart. Lift the shoulders up as high as you can to form a cradle round your head, hold for a second and return to a relaxed position. Do this 10 times.

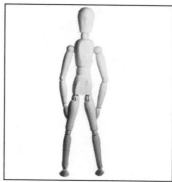

SIDE BEND

Stand with your feet a little more than hip-width apart with your toes pointing forwards and your hands by your sides. With your hand on the side of your thigh, bend towards the left so that you trace an imaginary trouser seam down the side of your leg. You must not lean forwards or backwards but flex sideways only. Slowly return to the upright position and do the exercise to the right. That counts as one repetition. This must be a smooth (not jerking) action rather like a stretching movement. Do the exercise 5 to 10 times.

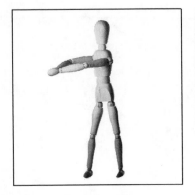

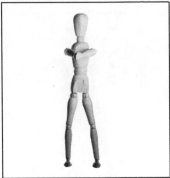

STANDING TWISTS

The aim of this exercise is to turn the lower spine/back without moving the hips. Link your hands in front of you, then lift your arms so that they are horizontal at shoulder level. Keeping your hips fixed, and with your knees slightly bent, turn your body to the left as far as you can in a con- 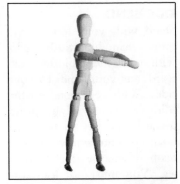 trolled smooth movement (not sudden or jerking) and return. Do the same to the right and back to the centre again. That counts as one repetition. Throughout the exercise, keep your hips in the fixed position facing forwards. Do the exercise 5 to 10 times.

SKI-PUSH ON THE SPOT

Stand upright with your feet hip-width apart and facing directly forwards. Lift your arms out in front of you so that your hands are level with your head. Pull the arms down and through a semi-circular motion, bending your knees and hips at the same time, as though you are pushing your-

self forwards on skis. Finish with your arms straight out behind you, then bring your arms forward and up again to return to the standing position. Make sure the movement is relaxed and smooth. You should be able to feel the tension in your thighs, calves and shoulders. Do the exercise 10 times.

In summary, the warm up exercises are:

	Exercise	Repetitions
1	Arm circling forwards and backwards	5 to 10 times forwards and 5 to 10 times backwards
2	Neck roll	5 to 10 times to the right and left alternately
3	Shoulder shrugs	10 times
4	Side bend	5 to 10 times to the right and left alternately
5	Standing twists	5 to 10 times to the right and left alternately
6	Ski-push on the spot	10 times

COOL-DOWN

Remember, by performing the exercises described above *in reverse order*, you can use this warm up routine as a cool-down routine.

EXERCISE TESTS

This is the main part of your fitness test. The following exercises will assess the fitness level of the four main areas of your body – legs, abdomen (or stomach), back and upper body. The results will be used to choose the exercises for your personal programme.

Before You Start:
o   Make sure that you have not eaten for at least one hour.

o   Wear exercise shoes/clothing if you have them. If not, wear clothing that does not restrict your freedom of movement.

o   If you have a serious injury then you must see your doctor or specialist before you attempt any of the exercises.

During The Test:

○ Move through the exercise tests in the sequence given. Level 1 first, then Levels 2 and 3 as far as they are appropriate to your ability. Rest for only a minute or so before moving on from one exercise to the next.

○ Read the exercise instructions carefully before you attempt each exercise and practise each movement two or three times to make sure you are comfortable and familiar with the exercise.

○ Perform each exercise test carefully and at a steady pace. Do not attempt to go as fast as possible. *Quality of exercise is far more important than quantity.*

○ If at any time during the test you feel ill, sick, dizzy, faint, sharp or repeated pain (especially in the chest) then stop immediately and seek specialist advice.

Before you start the test, make sure you have warmed up. Do the warm up exercises on pages 10–18.

TEST LEVEL I

You are now ready to start the tests. On Level 1, your goal is to do each of the following exercises 20 times without stopping. Stop if you feel discomfort; do not worry if you cannot do 20 repetitions and do not repeat each exercise more than 20 times.

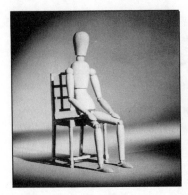 

LEGS: SQUAT FROM A CHAIR

This is primarily a leg exercise. If you have any kind of injury to any part of your leg please be very careful when you attempt this exercise.

Sit on a chair of average height (no more than about 25 inches high), keeping your feet a little wider than hip-width apart with your feet flat on the floor, toes pointing forwards and slightly outwards. Place your hands on your knees. Keeping your back straight and your head up, stand up from the chair to an upright position. As you stand up, move your arms (keeping them straight) from your knees to a horizontal position. Carefully sit down again and repeat the exercise.

Stop when you cannot do any more, but do not attempt more than 20 repetitions. Write the number of repetitions you have done in the Level 1 Legs box on the Test Exercises Chart on page 32. Rest for 1 minute or so, then practise the next exercise 2 or 3 times.

 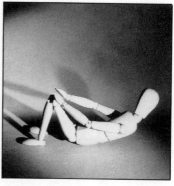

ABDOMINALS: WRIST-TO-KNEE SIT-UPS

This is primarily an abdomen exercise. If you have any kind of stomach/abdomen injury please be very careful when you attempt this exercise.

Lie down flat on your back and raise your knees so that they are approximately a foot off the floor, with your legs bent and together. Keeping your heels flat on the floor, stretch out your hands and place them on your thighs, palms down. Sit up gradually, curling your body and tucking the chin in to your chest so that you push your hands along your thighs to your knees. Stop where your natural body tension stops you or when your wrists touch your knees. Gently return to the starting position, sliding your hands back along your thighs. Repeat.

Stop when you cannot do any more, but do not attempt more than 20 repetitions. Write the number of repetitions you have done in the Level 1 Abdominals box on the Test Exercises Chart on page 32. Rest for 1 minute or so, then practise the next exercise 2 or 3 times.

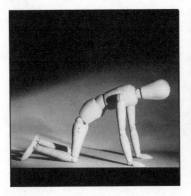 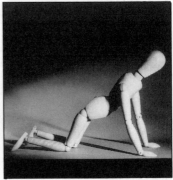

BACK: HUMP AND HOLLOW

This is primarily a back exercise. If you have any kind of back injury please be very careful when you attempt this exercise.

Adopt an all-fours position, so that you are equally balanced on both knees and both hands with your knees slightly apart, and hands slightly wider than shoulder-width apart. Arch your back up so that the back muscles are relaxed and the stomach muscles are tightened (hump). Then relax the stomach muscles and tighten the back muscles (hollow). Make sure you keep an equal balance on your hands and knees at all times during this exercise.

Stop when you cannot do any more, but do not attempt more than 20 repetitions. Write the number of repetitions you have done in the Level 1 Back box on the Test Exercises Chart on page 32. Rest for 1 minute or so, then practise the next exercise 2 or 3 times.

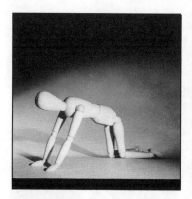 

UPPER BODY: PRESS-UPS, ALL FOURS

This is primarily an arm exercise. If you have any kind of arm/shoulder injury please be very careful when you attempt this exercise.

Adopt an all-fours position, equally balanced on your knees and hands, with your knees slightly apart, and toes on the floor. Keep your hands shoulder-width apart, with the fingers facing forwards. Tense your body and, keeping your back straight, lower yourself towards the floor, bending from your hips with knees on the ground until your face is 1–2 inches from the floor. Then press yourself back up again. Ensure you keep your back straight throughout this exercise.

Stop when you cannot do any more, but do not attempt more than 20 repetitions. Write the number of repetitions you have done in the Level 1 Upper Body box on the Test Exercises Chart on page 32. Rest for 1 minute or so, then practise the next exercise 2 or 3 times.

TEST LEVEL 2

On Level 2, you must attempt an exercise only if you managed to do 20 repetitions of the corresponding test on Level 1. Your goal on Level 2 is also to do each exercise 20 times at a steady pace without stopping. Do not worry if you cannot do 20 repetitions and do not repeat each exercise more than 20 times.

LEGS: HALF SQUATS

Attempt this exercise only if you performed 20 squats from a chair on Level 1.

Stand with your feet a little wider than hip-width apart and your toes pointing forwards and slightly outwards. Keeping your back straight and your head up, bend at the knees so that you sink into a squatting position with your thighs parallel to the ground. Keep your ankles down and your heels flat on the floor. Return to the standing position. Your centre of gravity should remain through the middle of your thighs throughout the movement and you should hold your hands so that they lightly touch the back of your head. If you find this difficult or painful, you can cross your arms and place them on your shoulders instead, or your arms can be held straight out in front of you. Try to keep your movements as smooth as possible throughout this exercise.

Stop when you cannot do any more, but do not do more than 20 repetitions in this or any other Level 2 exercise. Write the number of repetitions in the Level 2 Legs box on the Test Exercises Chart. Rest for 1 minute or so, then practise the next exercise 2 or 3 times.

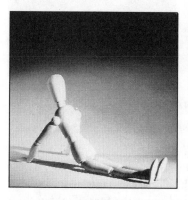 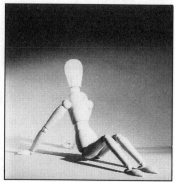

ABDOMINALS: LOWER ABDOMINAL CRUNCH, DOUBLE LEGS

Attempt this exercise only if you performed 20 wrist-to-knee sit-ups on Level 1.

Sit on the floor with your body leaning slightly back, supported by your hands behind your body with fingers pointing backwards, your legs stretched in front of you with the heels together. In one movement, lift and bend your legs and bring your knees in towards your chest as close to your buttocks as possible. Touch the ground with your heels, and then push the feet and legs straight out again, back to the starting position. It is important that the lower abdominal area is used and not the thigh muscles, so control the movement carefully.

Stop when you cannot do any more, but do not do more than 20 repetitions. Write the number of repetitions in the Level 2 Abdominal box on the Test Exercises Chart. Rest for 1 minute or so, then practise the next exercise 2 or 3 times.

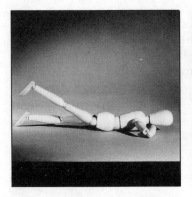 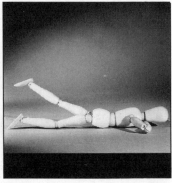

BACK: SINGLE-LEG BACK RAISE

Attempt this exercise only if you performed 20 hump and hollows on Level 1.

Lying flat on your front, clasp your hands under your chin so that your elbows are flat on the floor and your arms are flat. Keep your legs close together and point the toes. Tighten your buttocks and legs, and lift one leg off the floor from the hips so that your toes are 10 to 12 inches above the floor. Lower to the floor and repeat with the other leg. That counts as one repetition. Clench your buttocks before you lift your leg or you will throw the emphasis of the exercise on to your lower back.

Stop when you cannot do any more, but do not do more than 20 repetitions. Write the number of repetitions in the Level 2 Back box on the Test Exercises Chart. Rest for 1 minute or so, then practise the next exercise 2 or 3 times.

UPPER BODY: HALF PRESS-UPS

Attempt this exercise only if you performed 20 press-ups, all fours on Level I.

Adopt an all-fours position with your knees slightly apart. Keeping your hands fixed, move your knees backwards until your body is straight from knees to shoulders. Keep your hands a fraction more than shoulder-width apart, fingers facing forwards. Lower your upper body so that your arms take the weight, then lower your face to within 1 to 2 inches of the floor. Press back up to the starting position. Bend from the knees, keeping your knees on the floor and your back straight. You can make the exercise less or more difficult by moving your hands forwards or backwards.

Stop when you cannot do any more, but do not do more than 20 repetitions. Write the number of repetitions in the Level 2 Upper Body box on the Test Exercises Chart. Rest for 1 minute or so, then practise the next exercise 2 or 3 times.

TEST LEVEL 3

On Level 3, you must attempt an exercise only if you managed to do 20 repetitions of the corresponding test on Level 2. On Level 3 your goal is to complete *as many repetitions of each exercise as you can* at a steady pace without stopping. You must stop if you feel discomfort, sharp or repeated pain or if you feel ill, sick, dizzy or faint.

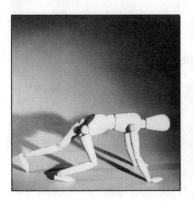 

LEGS: SINGLE-LEG SPRINTS

Attempt this exercise only if you performed 20 half squats on Level 2.

Support yourself on your hands and feet in the front-support position as though you were about to perform a full press-up. Bring one leg forward towards your chest, keeping the other leg straight. Now jump slightly and reverse the leg positions. Repeat this movement at a steady pace. Each time the right leg comes forward, it counts as one repetition. After you have completed as many as you can, stop and write the number of repetitions in the Level 3 Legs box on the Test Exercises Chart. Rest for 1 minute or so, then practise the next exercise 2 or 3 times.

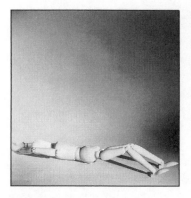 

ABDOMINALS: SIT-UPS THROUGH THE LEGS

Attempt this exercise only if you performed 20 lower abdominal crunches, double legs, on Level 2.

Lie flat on your back with your legs slightly bent, just a little more than hip-width apart, and with your arms stretched out behind your head on the floor. Bring your arms up over your head and then sit up, reaching forwards to touch the ground between your feet. Return to the starting position and repeat the exercise. Ensure that your hands touch the ground but not further forward than your feet. Try to keep the movement smooth and do not jerk your hands over your head. After you have completed as many as you can, write the number of repetitions in the Level 3 Abdominals on the Test Exercises Chart. Rest for 1 minute or so, then practise the next exercise 2 or 3 times.

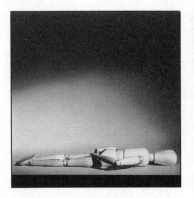 

BACK: BACK CURL, HANDS BEHIND

Attempt this exercise only if you performed 20 single-leg back raises on Level 2.

Lie flat with your face down and with the backs of your hands resting on your buttocks with your buttocks clenched. Keeping your legs down and your thighs on the ground (do not lift your thighs at all) raise your chest as high as possible off the floor so that the muscles in your back are tightened. Ensure that you keep your neck in line with your back throughout this exercise. Hold for a moment and then return to your original position. After you have completed as many as you can, write the total number of repetitions in the Level 3 Back box on the Test Exercises Chart. Rest for 1 minute or so, then practise the next exercise 2 or 3 times.

 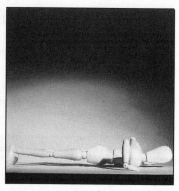

UPPER BODY: FULL PRESS-UPS

Attempt this exercise only if you performed 20 half press-ups on Level 2.

Adopt the front-support position, balancing on your hands and feet. Keep your body straight from your toe/ankle to your shoulder. Keep your hands just a fraction more than shoulder-width apart, with your fingers facing forwards. Lower your body, with your arms taking the full weight, until your face is within 1–2 inches off the floor. Press back up to the starting position. Ensure you keep your body straight the whole time. After you have completed this exercise as many times as you comfortably can, write the number of repetitions in the Level 3 Upper Body box on the Test Exercise Chart.

COOL DOWN NOW!

That completes the exercise tests. In order to return your body gently to its resting state, repeat the warm-up exercises described earlier *in reverse order*, to cool down.

TEST EXERCISES CHART

Record your exercise test scores below as you perform each test exercise:

LEGS

Level 1: **Squat from a chair** ☐

Level 2: **Half squats** ☐

Level 3: **Single-leg sprints** ☐

ABDOMINALS

Level 1: **Wrist-to-knee sit-ups** ☐

Level 2: **Lower abdominal crunch, double legs** ☐

Level 3: **Sit-ups through the legs** ☐

BACK

Level 1: **Hump and hollow** ☐

Level 2: **Single-leg back raise** ☐

Level 3: **Back curl, hands behind** ☐

UPPER BODY

Level 1: **Press-ups, all fours** ☐

Level 2: **Half press-ups** ☐

Level 3: **Full press-ups** ☐

HOW TO WORK OUT YOUR BODY LEVELS

On the chart, work through each of the four body areas above in turn.

○ Cross out any scores of fewer than 14 repetitions on any Level 2 and 3 exercise.

○ Your highest remaining scores determine your levels of fitness for each body area.

For example, if you scored 20 repetitions on the Level 1 exercise, 12 on the corresponding Level 2 exercise and 0 on the Level 3 exercise, you would cross out the scores of 0 and 12, leaving the Level 1 score. This would be your body level on that area.

○ As you go through each body area in turn, write in your body level (1, 2 or 3) in the body levels table below.

BODY LEVELS TABLE

Legs level	☐	(1, 2 or 3)
Abdominals level	☐	(1, 2 or 3)
Back level	☐	(1, 2 or 3)
Upper body level	☐	(1, 2 or 3)
Total score (sum of the above 4)	☐	= Total score (3 to 12)

DETERMINING YOUR OVERALL LEVEL

Look at your total score and body levels above and use the following simple rules to work out what your overall level is:

○ If your total score is 10 or above *and* you have no Level 1, your overall level is 3.
○ If your total score is 7 or below, your overall level is 1.
○ If you have two Level 1s, your overall level is 1.
○ If you fall into none of the above categories, your overall level is 2.

○ Write your overall level in the box below.

Overall level   ⬚ (1, 2 or 3)

HOW WELL DID YOU SCORE?

How well you scored depends mainly on your age and how much exercise you currently take:

○ If you are aged over 50, you probably achieved Level 1 scores.
○ If you are 35 to 50, you probably achieved Level 2 scores.
○ If you are under 35, you probably achieved Level 3 scores.
○ If you managed 21 or more repetitions on a Level 3 exercise, that is very good.
○ If you managed 41 or more repetitions on a Level 3 exercise, that is excellent.

Do not worry if you scored lower than average on the test because your Lifestyle Fitness Programme will take your scores into account however high or low they are. If you exercise at the right level, you will see your scores improve quite quickly.

YOUR PERSONAL FITNESS PROGRAMME

You are now going to use your test result scores to work out your personal fitness programme.

CHOOSING THE EXERCISES

The first step is to choose which exercises you are going to do. These are based on your body level scores from the exercise tests in chapter 2.

Look at your Personal Circuit Card on page 38. You will see that there are twelve exercises in total – three for each of the four body areas. For each body area, starting with legs, you choose the three exercises which are the correct level for you (see pages 41–72). So if you are a Legs Level 1, you choose the three Legs Level 1 exercises which are described at the end of this chapter. Repeat this for the abdominal, back and upper body exercises. *The set of twelve exercises you have chosen is your personal circuit.*

Write the names of the exercises on your personal circuit card. Later, in chapter 6, you will find more information on how to customize your programme even further to your personal needs.

CHOOSING THE REPETITIONS

The final step is to decide how many of each exercise to do. This is based on the overall level score that you calculated in chapter 2.

Look at the Repetitions Table below and choose the progression level which matches your Overall Level. For example, if your Overall Level is 2, then choose progression 2 and so on. Copy the number of repetitions for each of the 6 progression stages into the boxes on your personal circuit card now.

REPETITIONS TABLE

Stage	Progression 1	Progression 2	Progession 3
1	10	10 – 10	15 – 15
2	12	12 – 12	20 – 20
3	15	15 – 15	12 – 10 – 8
4	10 – 10	20 – 20	15 – 12 – 10
5	12 – 12	12 – 10 – 8	20 – 15 – 10
6	15 – 15	15 – 12 – 10	....

CONGRATULATIONS! YOU HAVE NOW DESIGNED YOUR OWN PERSONAL FITNESS PROGRAMME

Always start on stage 1 of your progression. For example, on stage 1 of progression 1, you perform each of the 12 exercises 10 times in order to make one exercise circuit. When you get fitter you will perform 12, then 15 repetitions of each exercise. On stage 4, you perform two circuits of 10 repetitions each.

The hardest stage is the last stage of progression 3 which is 20 – 15 – 10. This means performing each of the exercises, in order, 20 times. Then you go back to the top and perform each exercise 15 times again. Finally, go back to the top for a third time and perform each exercise again 10 times. That makes 3 circuits in total.

You do not take a rest between the circuits. In the last example above, you perform the three circuits one after the other without taking a rest.

HOW OFTEN TO EXERCISE AND HOW TO PROGRESS

Complete each stage at least four times (and no more than eight times) before you move up a stage. Do not attempt to move up through the stages more quickly. It will probably take you between one and two weeks to complete each stage.

Aim to exercise three times a week (two should be the minimum). However, since it only takes a few minutes, you may find it possible to complete the programme every day. The key is consistency. It is far better to exercise three times a week regularly than to exercise once one week and every day the next. Regular exercise helps the body adapt gradually to the slowly increasing workload.

Since you do not need any exercise equipment, you can perform the programme anywhere and at any time. There is nothing wrong with exercising late in the evening except that after raising your pulse, you may find it difficult to sleep.

PERSONAL CIRCUIT CHART

Specialization ▶

PERSONAL EXERCISE CIRCUIT

Area	Name of exercise	
Legs		UB
Abdominals		L
Back		A
Upper body		
Legs		UB
Abdominals		L
Back		A
Upper body		
Legs		UB
Abdominals		L
Back		A
Upper body		

REPETITIONS

Stage	Repetitions
1	
2	
3	
4	
5	
6	

EXERCISE NOTES

READ THROUGH THE FOLLOWING POINTS EACH TIME YOU EXERCISE

○ Perform the exercises one after the other, carefully and at a steady pace without stopping. Remember, the aim is *not* to finish the circuit in as fast a time as possible. The *quality* of the exercise you do is far more important than the speed or quantity.

○ Pause only momentarily and take care as you move between the different exercises, particularly if moving from a standing exercise to a floor-based exercise. At the end of a circuit, do not rest before going back up to the top again unless you feel you must.

○ Take your pulse for 15 seconds immediately after you have finished exercising and again for 15 seconds a minute later. Multiply these figures by 4 and make sure that your first pulse rate is between the two training limits from chapter 2.

○ Monitor your progress using the Progress Record on page 40.

○ Always warm up before you exercise and cool down after you exercise, using the routine described in chapter 2.

○ Never exercise if you feel ill or you are injured. If at any time during exercise you feel ill, sick, discomfort, dizziness, faintness, sharp or repeated pain (especially in the chest) then *stop immediately* and seek specialist or medical advice.

PROGRESS RECORD

Monitor your progress using this log:

1   The day and/or the date of the exercise session.
2   Which circuit and which stage you performed.
3   Tick after you have warmed up, to ensure that you warm up
     every time before you exercise.
     Always remember to cool down after exercising.
4   Take your pulse for 15 seconds immediately after exercising
     and 1 minute later.
     Multiply the figures by 4 to work out beats per minute.
     Make sure the first figure is within your safe pulse limits and
     that your pulse is falling quite quickly.
5   Record any other comments you have.

	1 Day & date	2 Circuit & stage	3 Warm up?	4 Pulses 1 & 2	5 Comments
1				–	
2				–	
3				–	
4				–	
5				–	
6				–	
7				–	
8				–	
9				–	
10				–	
11				–	
12				–	
13				–	
14				–	
15				–	

EXERCISE DESCRIPTIONS

For each of the four body areas, there are three levels of difficulty, each with three different exercises.

LEGS

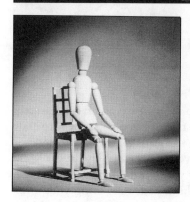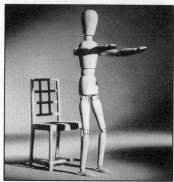

LEGS LEVEL 1: **SQUAT FROM A CHAIR**
Sit on a chair of average height (no more than about 25 inches
high), keeping your feet a little wider than hip-width apart with
your feet flat on the floor, toes pointing forwards and slightly
outwards. Place your hands on your knees. Keeping your back
straight and your head up, stand up from the chair to an upright
position. As you stand up, move your arms (keeping them
straight) from your knees to a horizontal position. Carefully sit
down again and repeat the exercise.

LEGS LEVEL 1: **SKI-PUSH ON THE SPOT**

Stand upright with your feet hip–width apart and facing directly forwards. Lift your arms out in front of you so that your hands are level with your head. Pull the arms down and through a semi–circular motion, bending your knees and hips at the same time, as though you are pushing yourself forward on skis. Finish with your arms straight out behind you, then bring your arms forward and up again to return to the standing position. Make sure the movement is relaxed and smooth. You should be able to feel the tension in your thighs, calves and shoulders.

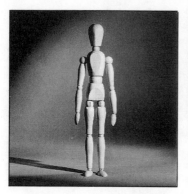 

LEGS LEVEL 1: **JUMPING JACKS**

Stand with your feet together and your arms by your sides. Jump so that your feet are apart, landing lightly on your toes with your arms straight out to the sides at shoulder height. As you land, jump straight back to the starting position again. Repeat continuously for the prescribed number of repetitions.

LEGS LEVEL 2: **HALF SQUATS**

Stand with your feet a little wider than hip–width apart and your toes pointing forwards and slightly outwards. Keeping your back straight and your head up, bend at the knees so that you sink into a squatting position with your thighs parallel to the ground. Keep your ankles down and your heels flat on the floor. Return to the standing position. Your centre of gravity should remain through the middle of your thighs throughout the movement and you should hold your hands so that they lightly touch the back of your head. If you find this difficult or painful, you can cross your arms and place them on your shoulders instead, or your arms can be held straight out in front of you. Try to keep your movements as smooth as possible throughout this exercise.

LEGS LEVEL 2: **LUNGES**

Stand with your feet hip-width apart and your toes pointing forwards. Take a long step forwards with one leg and hold the position with your legs astride. Keeping your head up and your back straight, gently bring your weight down on the forward leg, bending the knee until your thigh is parallel to the floor. In this position the knee of your back leg will also be slightly bent. Push up from the front leg back to the starting position with your feet hip-width apart, then repeat the movement with the other leg forward. That counts as one repetition.

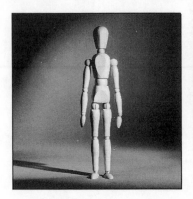

LEGS LEVEL 2: **JUMPING JACKS**

Stand with your feet together and your arms by your side. Jump so that your feet are apart, landing lightly on your toes with your arms straight out to the sides at shoulder height. As you land, jump straight back to the starting position again. Repeat continuously for the prescribed number of repetitions.

LEGS LEVEL 3: **SINGLE-LEG SPRINTS**

Support yourself on your hands and feet in the front-support position as though you were about to perform a full press-up. Bring one leg forward towards your chest, keeping the other leg straight. Now jump slightly and reverse the leg positions. Repeat this movement at a steady pace. Each time the right leg comes forwards, it counts as one repetition. Rest for 1 minute or so, then practise the next exercise 2 or 3 times.

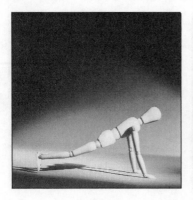 

LEGS LEVEL 3: **SQUAT THRUSTS**

Support yourself on your hands and feet with your back straight, as if you were about to perform a full press-up. Bring both legs up towards your chest in a jumping movement so that the knees touch the elbows, before springing back immediately to the straight position. Some people will find they are flexible enough to allow their knees to come inside their elbows. Others are more comfortable with their knees on the outside. Either will do. Repeat the movement continuously at a steady pace.

LEGS LEVEL 3: **HINGES FROM FLOOR**

Kneel on the floor (with feet flat) with your knees together and with your buttocks resting on your heels. Keeping your weight back and using your thighs only, kneel up and then forward until your thighs are vertical. Then, still using your thighs, lower yourself slowly back to the start position. Be sure to keep your back straight and your head up the whole time during this exercise.

ABDOMINALS

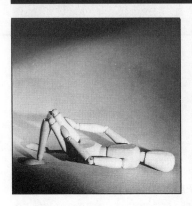
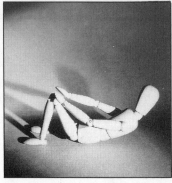

ABDOMINALS LEVEL I: **WRIST-TO-KNEE SIT-UPS**

Lie down flat on your back and raise your knees so that they are approximately a foot off the floor, with your legs bent and together. Keeping your heels flat on the floor, stretch out your hands and place them on your thighs, palms down. Sit up gradually, curling your body and tucking the chin into your chest so that you push your hands along your thighs to your knees. Stop where your natural body tension stops you or when your wrists touch your knees. Gently return to the starting position, sliding your hands back along your thighs. Repeat.

ABDOMINALS LEVEL I: **SIT-UPS, HANDS ON SHOULDERS**

Lie down flat on your back and raise your knees so that your heels are on the ground close to your buttocks, with your knees bent and together. Keeping your feet flat on the floor, cross your arms and place your hands on the opposite shoulders. Sit up gradually, curling your body and tucking your chin into your chest. Finish at the point where your natural body tension stops you, or when you are upright. Then gently return to the starting position.

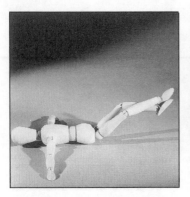 

ABDOMINALS LEVEL 1:
KNEES TO CHEST

Lie flat on your back with your hands in a comfortable position out from your body, palms down. Now cross your feet and raise your legs off the floor, with your knees slightly bent. Using the lower abdominal muscles, curl your thighs towards your chest so that your buttocks just lift off the floor. Return to the start position (knees slightly bent) and repeat.

 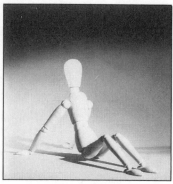

ABDOMINALS LEVEL 2:
LOWER ABDOMINAL CRUNCH, DOUBLE LEGS

Sit on the floor with your body leaning slightly back, supported by your hands behind your body with fingers pointing backwards, your legs stretched in front of you with the heels together. In one movement, lift and bend your legs and bring your knees in towards your chest as close to your buttocks as possible. Touch the ground with your heels, and then push the feet and legs straight out again, back to the starting position. It is important that the lower abdominal area is used and not the thigh muscles, so control the movement carefully.

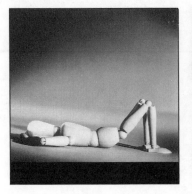 

ABDOMINALS LEVEL 2: **SIT-UPS, HANDS ON EARS**

Lie down flat on your back and raise your knees so that your heels are on the ground close to your buttocks, with your knees bent and together. Keeping your feet flat on the floor, place your hands lightly on your head behind your ears, with your elbows out to the side. Sit up gradually, curling your body and tucking the chin into your chest. Finish where your natural body tension stops you, or when you are upright. Gently return to the starting position. Keep your hands lightly touching your head behind the ears throughout. Do *not* lock your hands together or apply any pressure to your head with your hands.

 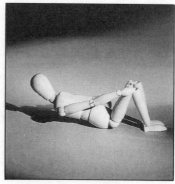

ABDOMINALS LEVEL 2: **SIT-UPS, HAND PAST KNEE**

Lie flat on your back with knees raised and heels on the ground close to your buttocks. Now gradually sit up, curling your body to reach your right hand past your right knee. Return to the starting position and repeat, but this time reaching the left hand past your left knee. That counts as one repetition.

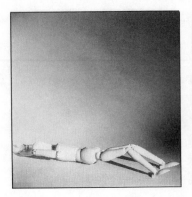 

ABDOMINALS LEVEL 3: **SIT-UPS THROUGH THE LEGS**

Lie flat on your back with your legs slightly bent, just a little more than hip–width apart, and with your arms stretched out behind your head on the floor. Bring your arms up over your head and then sit up, reaching forwards to touch the ground between your feet. Return to the starting position and repeat the exercise. Ensure that your hands touch the ground but not further forward than your feet. Try to keep the movement smooth and do not jerk your hands over your head.

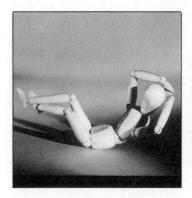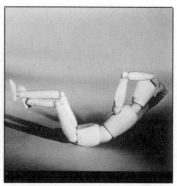

ABDOMINALS LEVEL 3:
HALF ABDOMINAL CRUNCH, ALTERNATE

Lie on your back on the floor. Bring your feet up so they are on the ground as close to your buttocks as possible, with your thighs vertical. Cross your feet and curl your knees towards your chest so that your feet are in the air and your buttocks are raised slightly off the ground. This is the start position. Place your hands lightly on your head behind your ears but do not apply any pressure to your head. Bring your right elbow up towards your left knee so that you can feel a 'crunching' motion on your abdominal muscles. Return to the start, then bring your left elbow up towards your right knee. That counts as one repetition.

ABDOMINALS LEVEL 3: **SALMON SNAP**

Lie flat on your back, arms outstretched behind your head. Swiftly bring both arms over your head and raise one leg (keeping it straight) so that your hands meet your foot in a V. Return to the floor and repeat the exercise with the other leg raised. That counts as one repetition.

BACK

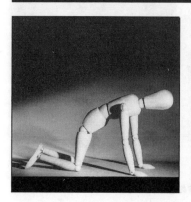 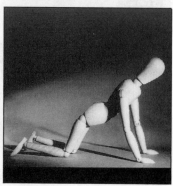

BACK LEVEL 1: **HUMP AND HOLLOW**

Adopt an all-fours position, so that you are equally balanced on both knees and both hands with your knees slightly apart, and hands slightly wider than shoulder-width apart. Arch your back up so that the back muscles are relaxed and the stomach muscles are tightened (hump). Then relax the stomach muscles and tighten the back muscles (hollow). Make sure you keep an equal balance on your hands and knees at all times during this exercise.

 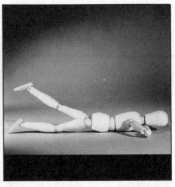

BACK LEVEL 1 : **SINGLE-LEG BACK RAISE**

Lying flat on your front, clasp your hands under your chin so that your elbows are on the floor and your arms are flat. Keep your legs close together and point your toes. Now tighten your buttocks and legs, and lift one leg off the floor from the hip so that toes are approximately 10 to 12 inches off the floor. Return to the starting position and repeat with the other leg. That counts as one repetition. Make sure that your buttocks are clenched and tightened before you lift your leg, otherwise you will throw the emphasis of the exercise on to your lower back.

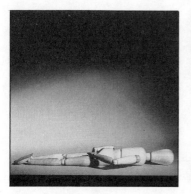 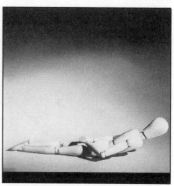

BACK LEVEL 1: **BACK CURL**

Lie on the floor, face down with the backs of your hands resting on your buttocks and with your buttocks clenched. Keeping your legs down and your thighs on the floor (do not lift your thighs at all during the exercise), raise your chest as high as you possibly can off the floor so that the muscles in your back are tightened. Ensure that you keep your neck in line with your back throughout the exercise. Do not attempt to raise your chest past the point at which it starts to feel uncomfortable. Return to the start position.

BACK LEVEL 2: **SINGLE-LEG BACK RAISE**

Same as Back Level 1: Single-leg back raise. See description opposite.

BACK LEVEL 2: **BACK CURL, HANDS BEHIND**

Same as Back Level 1: Back curl, hands behind. See description above.

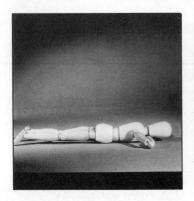 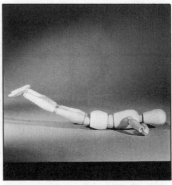

BACK LEVEL 2: **DOUBLE-LEG BACK RAISE**

Lying flat on your front, clasp your hands under your head so that your elbows and arms are flat on the floor. Keep your legs close together and point the toes. Now tighten your buttocks and legs, and lift both legs off the floor from the hips so that the toes are approximately 10 to 12 inches off the floor. Return to the start position. Make sure that your buttocks are clenched and tightened before you raise your legs, otherwise you will throw the emphasis of the exercise on to your lower back.

BACK LEVEL 3: **BACK CURL**

Same as Back Level 1: Back curl, hands behind. See description above.

BACK LEVEL 3: **DOUBLE LEG BACK RAISE**

Same as Back Level 2: Double leg back raise. See description above.

BACK LEVEL 3: **ALTERNATE ARM/LEG THRUSTS**

Start in an all-fours position on your hands and knees. Move the right leg from the bent position and thrust it out behind you, pointing the toe. At the same time extend the left arm in front of you. The leg and arm should be straight, parallel with the floor. Return to the start position and repeat with the left leg and right arm. That counts as one repetition.

UPPER BODY

UPPER BODY LEVEL 1: **PRESS-UPS, ALL FOURS**

Adopt an all-fours, equally balanced position on your knees and hands, with your knees slightly apart, and toes on the floor. Keep your hands shoulder-width apart with the fingers facing forwards. Tense your body and, keeping your back straight, lower yourself towards the floor, bending from your hips with knees on the ground until your face is 1 to 2 inches from the floor. Then press yourself back up again. Ensure you keep your back straight throughout this exercise.

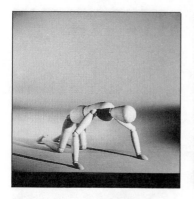 

UPPER BODY LEVEL I: **PRESS-UPS, ALL FOURS WIDE**

Adopt an all-fours position so that you are equally balanced on both knees and both hands with your knees slightly apart. Place your hands about 1 foot wider than shoulder-width, with your fingers facing forwards. Tense your body and lower yourself towards the floor. Keep your back straight and bend from your hips with your knees on the ground until your face is within 1 to 2 inches of the floor. Then press yourself back up to the starting position.

UPPER BODY LEVEL 1 : **ARM EXTENSION**

Adopt the front support position as if for a full press-up, balancing on your hands and toes. Your hands should be just a fraction more than shoulder-width apart. Keeping every muscle taut and your arms and back straight, lift your hips up into the air and bring your head through your arms. Return to the front support position and repeat.

UPPER BODY LEVEL 2: **HALF PRESS-UPS**

Adopt an all-fours position with your knees slightly apart. Keeping your hands fixed, move your knees backwards until your body is straight from knees to shoulders. Keep your hands a fraction more than shoulder-width apart, fingers facing forwards. Lower your upper body so that your arms take the weight, then lower your face to within 1 to 2 inches of the floor. Press back up to the starting position. Bend from the knees, keeping your knees on the floor and your back straight. You can make the exercise less or more difficult by moving your hands forwards or backwards.

UPPER BODY LEVEL 2: **HALF PRESS-UPS, NARROW**

Adopt an all-fours, equally balanced position on both knees and both hands, with your knees slightly apart. Move your knees backwards until your body makes a straight line from your knees to your shoulders. Keep your hands about 6 inches apart, fingers facing forwards. Lower the body, with your arms taking the full weight, until your face is 1 to 2 inches from the floor. Now press back up to the starting position. Keep your body straight the whole time, bending from the knees and keeping your knees on the floor. You can make the exercise less or more difficult by moving your knees forwards or backwards to suit your ability.

UPPER BODY LEVEL 2: **ARM EXTENSION, WIDE**

Adopt the front support position as if for a full press-up, balancing on your hands and toes. Your hands should be approximately 1 foot more than shoulder-width apart. Keeping every muscle in your body taut and your arms and back straight, lift your hips up into the air and bring your head through your arms. Return to the front support position and repeat.

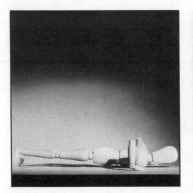 

UPPER BODY LEVEL 3: **FULL PRESS-UPS**

Adopt the front-support position, balancing on your hands and feet. Keep your body straight from your toe/ankle to your shoulder. Keep your hands just a fraction more than shoulder-width apart, with your fingers facing forwards. Lower your body, with your arms taking the full weight, until your face is within 1 to 2 inches of the floor. Press back up to the starting position. Ensure you keep your body straight the whole time. After you have completed this exercise as many times as you comfortably can, enter the number of repetitions in the Level 3: Upper body box in the Test Exercises Chart.

UPPER BODY LEVEL 3: **FULL PRESS-UPS, WIDE**

Adopt the front support position as if for a full press-up. Keeping your body straight from toe/ankle to shoulder, widen your hand support so that your hands are wider than your shoulder-width by about 1 foot, with your fingers facing forwards. Lower your body, with your arms taking the full weight, until your face is within 1 to 2 inches of the floor. Now press back up to the starting position. Make sure you keep your body straight the whole time.

UPPER BODY LEVEL 3: **ARM EXTENSION, ONE ARM**
Adopt the front support position as if for a full press-up, balancing on your hands and toes. Balancing on one arm, place the other behind your back. Keeping every muscle taut and your arms and back straight, raise your hips and bring your head past your supporting arm. Return to the start and repeat. When you have completed the required number of repetitions on one arm, change arms and repeat.

GETTING THE MEASURE OF YOUR FAT

This chapter focuses on your shape and enables you to work out whether you are overweight, what percentage of your body is fat and how much weight you should lose. It is not essential that you read this chapter and it does not affect your personal programme.

To complete the following tests, you will need a tape measure, gradated in inches, and an electronic calculator to perform some of the calculations.

We start by taking several physical measurements with a tape measure. These will help you work out the amount of fat you are carrying on your body and you will see the changes as you follow your programme. When measuring:

○ The tape measure should be taut and snug but should *not* cut the skin.

○ If you are right-handed take the measurements on the left-hand side of your body and vice versa.

○ Always measure from the same side (for example, do not measure your left bicep one week and the right one the next) because your limbs are slightly different sizes.

Go through each measurement, following the instructions and transferring the figures to the **physical measurements table** below.

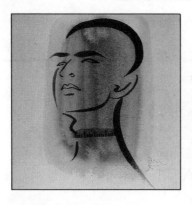

Neck
Measure your neck just below
the larynx or Adam's apple.

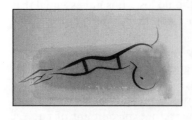

Upper arm (biceps)
Measure the thickest part of
the biceps/triceps muscle
group with your arm held out
from your body and your
palm facing down. Make sure
you keep your arm straight
and held at a 90-degree angle
to your body.

Lower arm (forearm)
Continue to hold your arm
straight from your shoulder

with palm facing down, and
measure the largest part of
your forearm.

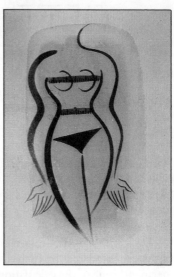

Expanded
chest measurement
The measurement is taken
round the height of the nipples
while you take the deepest
possible breath and fully
expand your chest.

Waist (abdomen)
Measure at the level of the
navel. During the measurement, stand evenly on both
legs and hold the stomach in a
normal relaxed position – *not*
sucked in.

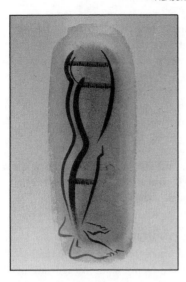

Hips
The measurement is taken round the widest part of the buttocks.

Thigh
Stand evenly on both legs with your feet apart. Measure just below the buttocks at the top of one leg.

Calf
Measure the thickest part of your calf. Take care when bending down if you suffer from back problems.

PHYSICAL MEASUREMENTS TABLE

Measurement	Inches
Neck	
Upper arm	
Lower arm	
Expanded chest	
Waist	
Hips	
Thigh	
Calf	

Monitor how these measurements change over time as you get fitter by taking the measurements again periodically.

Remember to measure your progress in inches as well as pounds.

WAIST-TO-HIPS RATIO

It is not simply the amount of fat you carry that is important. What also matters is where the fat is distributed. Men tend to carry excess fat on their bellies whilst women tend to deposit it on their thighs and hips. Arms and back can also be significant fat depositories.

Several studies have shown that a high waist-to-hips ratio is strongly associated with coronary heart and artery disease, stroke and other causes of premature death. Write your physical measurements into the boxes below and divide the figures to calculate your waist-to-hips ratio.

Waist (inches)	**Hips** (inches)		
/		=	Waist-to-Hips Ratio

In men, the risk of heart disease and stroke increases when the waist-to-hips ratio rises above **1.0**, and in women, when it rises above **0.8**. In either cases this may be a sign of fatness.

CHEST–WAIST DIFFERENCE

There should be a substantial difference between your expanded chest and your waist measurements. Write your measurements in the boxes below and subtract waist from chest to find your chest–waist difference.

Chest (inches)	**Waist** (inches)		
–		=	Chest–waist difference

For women, the difference should be at least **10** inches and for men it should be at least **5** inches. If your difference is less than this, it may be an indication that you should lose fat.

PINCHING AN INCH

At least half of your body fat is directly under your skin, so these simple pinch tests can help give you a rough estimate of the amount of fat you are carrying on your body. A pinch measurement of between half to one inch for each site is quite acceptable. Less than half an inch is low and more than 1 inch is a sign of fatness.

○   If you are right-handed take the pinches from your left-hand side and vice versa.

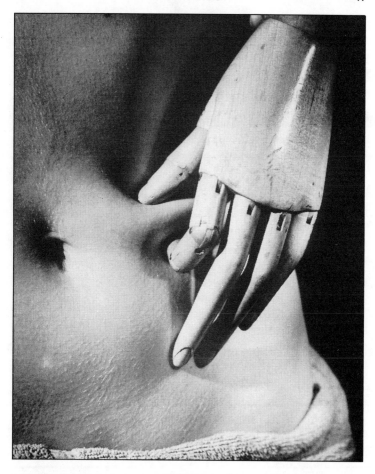

○   Stand in a relaxed position when taking each test and also
    ensure that you relax the area where you are taking the pinch
    from (clenching your muscles is cheating).

○   Do not take measurements through any clothing.

○   When taking a pinch, place your thumb and forefinger two
    to three inches apart, then pull the enclosed area together
    and hold firmly to measure the thickness of the fold *between*
    your thumb and forefinger.

○   You take three pinch measurements which are from different places for men and women. Follow the instructions carefully to ensure that you take the correct three measurements.

MEN

○ Chest – half-way along the line between the nipple and the armpit.

○ Abdomen – one inch either side of the navel.

○ Thigh – place your leg one step forward then take the pinch half-way along the top of the thigh, between the top of the knee cap and the hip. The pinch must be made in line with the thigh bone.

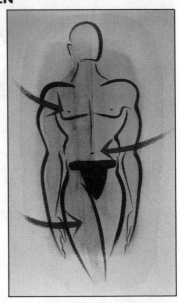

As you take these pinch tests, write your measurements in the boxes below:

MEN Area	**Pinch measurement** (inches)
Chest	
Abdomen	
Thigh	
Total (inches)	

WOMEN

The three sites for women are:

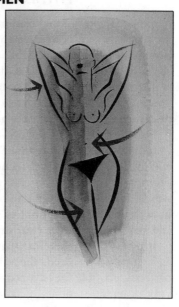

○ Upper arm – on the back of the upper arm, half-way between the elbow and the shoulder joint. The pinch must be made along the line of the arm bone (you will need some-one to help you take this measurement).

○ Waist – one inch above the hip bone, to the side of the body.

○ Thigh – place your leg one step forward then take the pinch half-way along the top of the thigh, between the top of the knee cap and the hip. The pinch must be made in line with the thigh bone.

As you take these pinch tests, write your measurements in the boxes below:

WOMEN Area	**Pinch measurement** (inches)
Upper arm	
Waist	
Thigh	
Total (inches)	

FATNESS AND WEIGHT

It is easy to confuse the relationship between weight and fat and *say* that a person is overweight when what is *meant* is that the person should lose fat. Most men and women are concerned about their appearance and so the amount of fat they are carrying is important. In addition, research has indicated that the fatter you are, the higher your chance of contracting coronary heart disease and a number of other health-related problems.

Lean body tissue is the non-fat part of your body composed of muscle, bones and organs. These are the tissues which require energy (or calories) to function. Your fat doesn't need any calories because it *is* excess calories that have already been stored. It is the weight of lean body tissue that is more important in determining the amount of energy you need during the day and how many calories you burn during exercise.

It is easy to see therefore that although an individual's weight and fatness are related, they are not necessarily the same. It is perfectly possible for two people to weigh the same but to have very different amounts of fat and lean body tissue. However, although weight and fatness are not perfectly related it is still useful to know whether you are overweight.

ARE YOU OVERWEIGHT?

A proven method of establishing whether you are overweight is to calculate your Body Mass Index from the figures for your weight (in kilos) and your height (in metres). Unlike the other measurements in this test, these measurements have to be metric in order to apply the following formula.

First, you need to work out your height in metres. To convert inches to metres multiply your height in inches by 2.54 and divide by 100. For example, 68 inches (5 feet 8 inches) × 2.54 ÷ 100 = 1.73 metres.

Secondly, you need to work out your weight in kilos. To convert pounds to kilos divide your weight in pounds by 2.2. For example, 147 pounds (10 stone 7 pounds) / 2.2 = 66.8 kilos. When you weigh yourself, always use scales as accurate as possible (for example the ones usually found in sports centres) and always use the same scales.

To work out your Body Mass Index, calculate the square of your height in metres by multiplying your height by itself. For example, the square of 1.73 is 2.99 (1.73 × 1.73). Write this figure and your weight in kilos in the boxes below and divide them for your score.

Weight (kilos)		**Height** × height			
66.8	/	2.99	=	22.3	example
	/	.	=		body mass index

The example above shows a person who is 1.73 metres tall (5 feet 8 inches) and weighs 66.8 kilos (10 stone 7 pounds). Their body mass index (BMI) is 22.3. Once you have worked your BMI out, check your score in the table below:

BODY MASS INDEX (BMI) TABLE

BMI	Category
40 +	Obese
30 – 39.9	Very overweight
25 – 29.9	Overweight
20 – 24.9	Acceptable weight
0 – 19.9	Underweight

The body mass index is only an estimate of how overweight you are. It is still perfectly possible for a muscular individual or an individual with a large body-frame to appear overweight in the table without being fat. Similarly, it is possible for an individual to be quite fat yet appear within the acceptable weight range.

You can get further indications of your level of fatness by considering your pinch measurements, your chest–waist difference and your waist-to-hips ratio. Follow these steps to calculate your Fat Points score:

○ For every pinch measurement that was greater than 1 inch, add 1 point.

○ If you are *male* and the sum of your pinch measurements was 3 inches or more, add 1 point.

○ If you are *male* and your chest–waist difference was less than 5 inches, add 1 point.

○ If you are *male* and your waist-to-hips ratio was more than 1.0, add 1 point.

○ If you are *female* and the sum of your pinch measurements was 4 inches or more, add 1 point.

○ If you are *female* and your chest–waist difference was less than 10 inches, add 1 point.

○ If you are *female* and your waist-to-hips ratio was more than 0.8, add 1 point.

How many Fat Points have your scored?

Fat Points

CALCULATING YOUR BODY FAT PERCENTAGE

To find out what percentage of your body is fat (body fat percentage), look up your fat points score and your body mass index category in the table below:

MEN Fat points ▼	▶body mass index	Underweight	Acceptable	Overweight	Very overweight or obese
0		10%	15%	15%	20%
1 or 2		15%	20%	20%	25%
3 or 4		15%	25%	25%	30%
5 or 6		20%	30%	30%	35%

For example, if you are a man, scored in the overweight category of the body mass index table and your fat point score is 2, your estimated body fat percentage is 20 per cent.

WOMEN Fat points ▼	▶body mass index	Underweight	Acceptable	Overweight	Very overweight or obese
0		15%	20%	20%	25%
1 or 2		20%	25%	25%	30%
3 or 4		20%	30%	30%	35%
5 or 6		25%	35%	35%	40%

For example, if you are a woman, scored in the acceptable category of the body mass index table and your fat point score is 3, your estimated body fat percentage is 30 per cent.

HOW MUCH FAT SHOULD YOU LOSE?

The acceptable body fat percentages are 20 and below for men and 25 and below for women. To calculate the weight of fat you are carrying, and how much of it you should lose, start by multiplying your weight in kilos by your body fat percentage and dividing by 100:

Weight (kilos)		Body fat percentage			
60	×	25	/ 100 =	15	example
	×		/ 100 =		actual kilos of fat

For example, if you weigh 60 kilos and have 25% body fat, you are carrying 15 kilos of fat.

Next, calculate the ideal maximum number of fat kilos you should be carrying, by multiplying your weight in kilos by a Fat Factor of *0.17* for men or *0.22* for women.

Weight (kilos)		Fat factor		
	×		=	ideal kilos of fat

Finally, to calculate approximately how much fat you should lose, subtract your ideal kilos of fat from your actual.

Ideal kilos of fat		Actual kilos of fat		
	−		=	kilos of fat (or weight) to lose

Please remember that without using specialist equipment, these figures can only be rough estimates. If your result is zero or less than zero then you are already at or below the ideal fat percentage.

Because muscle is denser than fat, the amount of weight you will have to lose will actually be slightly less than this because as you exercise you will burn off fat but gain muscle.

HEART – AEROBIC FITNESS

Aerobic exercise is very important. In the Sixties it was proved that twenty minutes of aerobic exercise three times a week had a significantly beneficial effect on the fitness of the heart, lungs and circulatory system – the very body systems which keep you alive. It improves stamina and effectively burns off fat. The longer the activity, the more fat is burned.

If your exercise circuit takes you fifteen minutes or more (not including your warm-up and cool-down) *and* you perform your circuit three times a week or more then you are getting all the aerobic exercise you need. However, if you have not yet reached a level where your circuit takes fifteen minutes to complete, or you complete your circuit fewer than three times per week, you need to take some additional aerobic exercise.

Although aerobics classes are an example of an aerobic activity, the two should not be confused. 'Aerobic' (literally 'with oxygen') activities are those which *continuously* keep your pulse raised for several (usually twenty or more) minutes. During aerobic exercise, your muscles and heart need more oxygen which must be collected by your lungs and distributed by your circulatory system. Brisk walks, jogging, running, rowing, vigorous dancing (e.g. disco or aerobics classes), cycling and swimming are good examples. Short explosive activities such as sprinting or discus-throwing are not aerobic.

Most common sports such as tennis, football and squash have some aerobic benefit depending on how vigorously the sport is played and for how long. For example, in professional football a midfield player would probably have a fair aerobic fitness level because he has to spend much of the game running, but a goalkeeper would have a very low aerobic capacity. However, because the activity is not continuous, even the midfield player may not get as much aerobic exercise as you might think. The key thing is to raise your pulse *continuously* for twenty minutes to get an aerobic benefit.

MEASURING YOUR AEROBIC FITNESS

Do not attempt this test if you have a heart condition, or you suffer from angina or pains in the chest.

The step test below will give you a good indication of your aerobic or cardiovascular fitness. You will need a step about 10 inches high (do *not* use a chair or a piece of furniture) and a watch with a second hand. You are also going to need to check your pulse, so make sure you are familiar with taking your pulse (see chapter 2).

You should do a short pre-test to confirm that the step test is safe for you. You will need a flight of stairs with 12 to 15 steps. Walk up it *at normal speed*, then down again. Do this three times without resting, then take your pulse for 15 seconds. If it is over 40, or your feel pain (especially chest pain), numbness, dizziness or are out of breath, do not attempt the step test and consult your GP or specialist. If you do not have a suitable staircase, jog on the spot fairly energetically for 45 seconds.

THE STEP TEST

The stepping movement is in four stages, each cycle beginning and ending with both feet on the floor. Time your steps at a rate of one complete cycle every two seconds (30 cycles per minute) for **four minutes** without stopping. Maintain a smooth 'step-up-step-down' movement throughout.

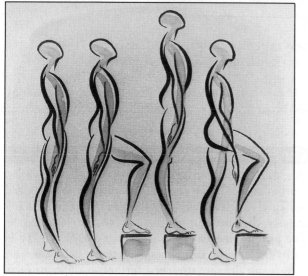

= I cycle

When you have finished, rest for one minute then take your pulse for 15 seconds. Rest for another 45 seconds and take your pulse again for 15 seconds. Rest for 45 seconds more and again take your pulse for 15. Write the counts in the boxes below and multiply by four to calculate the beats per minute.

Exercise pulses	Beats in 15 seconds	Beats per minute
1	× 4 =	
2	× 4 =	
3	× 4 =	
	Total beats	

Transfer the total into the box below and divide 24,000 by the figure to give you your result.

	Total beats		
24,000	/	=	Result

Rating: Less than 61 = poor; 61–70 = average; 71–80 = good; 81–90 = very good; more than 90 = excellent.

You should take the step test again from time to time during your fitness programme to monitor your rate of improvement.

AEROBIC EXERCISE PROGRAMMES

The three programmes in this section – swimming, walking and jogging/walking – are suitable for a wide range of abilities but are particularly designed for individuals with a low aerobic ability. The programmes will increase your aerobic ability in easy stages by building up to a twenty-minute period of aerobic exercise which can then be stretched further to thirty to forty minutes, if you wish.

You can combine your circuit and your aerobic exercise programme on the same day by performing the aerobic exercise just before your circuit.

CHOOSING AN ACTIVITY

Your step-test score helps determine which aerobic activity you should choose. If you scored poorly or you are over 40, you should not start with the jogging programme. If you have an injury (particularly a back injury) you must also not attempt the jogging programme but try swimming instead.

Remember to take your pulse after aerobic exercise just as you do after an exercise circuit. Always warm up before you exercise and cool down afterwards.

SWIMMING PROGRAMME

Swimming is very good for all-round fitness. Of all the aerobic activities, it places the least stress on your body because your body weight is supported by the water. It is particularly suitable for people with back or leg injuries, though anyone with a back (or neck) injury should avoid the breast-stroke.

Preliminary Stage
See how many minutes you can swim continuously at a moderate pace up to a maximum of twenty minutes. If you can swim for twenty minutes continuously, go straight to Stage 2.

Stage 1
Start by swimming for the number of minutes you recorded in the preliminary stage. Then, every four to six times you visit the pool, add two minutes to the total time you swim. Do not swim faster or more vigorously, concentrate instead on building up the time you swim to twenty minutes.

Swim the first two lengths slightly slower than normal and gradually build up to full speed to allow your body to warm up.

Stage 2
Record how many lengths you can swim in twenty minutes. Your goal is to start to swim more vigorously to increase the distance you cover. Do not attempt to do a fixed distance in a shorter time. You will see quite a difference in the distance you can swim for the first few times you try this, but improvements will become harder to achieve as you swim more often. When you register no improvement for three consecutive sessions, move up to Stage 3.

Stage 3

You can now choose how you progress further. You may:

a   Vary your stroke. For example, you could alternate three lengths of breast-stroke with one of crawl.

or b   Add a further two minutes to the total time every four to six times you swim, up to a maximum of thirty minutes.

or c   Vary your speed: you could try swimming three lengths at a steady pace, alternating with single lengths at a fast pace for the duration of your session.

WALKING PROGRAMME

Walking is a very good fitness activity provided you walk *briskly* (which raises your pulse). Walking briskly means walking as fast as you comfortably can without feeling you need to break into a jog. Walking at this speed has all the benefits of jogging/running but without the increased danger of strains or injury.

Always remember to warm up before you start, using the warm-up routine in chapter 2, and cool down after walking following the exercises in the routine in reverse order.

Ensure that you walk in suitable *flat-soled* shoes such as training shoes or special cross-training shoes, *not* in shoes that have heels (consult a good sports shop for further advice).

Preliminary Stage

Wearing flat training shoes, see how long you can walk continuously *and briskly*, up to a maximum of twenty minutes. *You must walk briskly, not stroll.* If you can do twenty minutes, go straight to Stage 2.

Stage 1

Start by walking for the number of minutes you recorded in the preliminary stage. Divide your time in half, walking out for the first half of the time and back for the second half. This helps you to cover the entire distance at a constant speed. Walk the first two or three minutes slightly slower to warm up; similarly, the last two or three minutes to cool down. Every four to six times you go walking, add two minutes to your total time (one minute out and one minute back), aiming to build up to an eventual maximum of twenty minutes.

Stage 2

Record how far you can walk in twenty minutes. Now you can walk continuously for this length of time, you should begin to walk faster to build up the distance. Always walk for twenty minutes. Do not attempt a set distance in a shorter time. Remember to walk out for the first ten minutes and back for the second ten minutes and walk for the first two or three minutes at a slightly slower speed to warm up. Once you have walked three consecutive sessions without improving the distance, move up to Stage 3.

Stage 3

You can now decide how to progress further. You may:

a   Add a further two minutes to the total time every four to six times you walk, up to a maximum of thirty minutes.

or b   Increase the intensity by walking up hills, pumping your arms more vigorously or carrying specially designed light hand-weights which will improve the muscle tone in your upper body.

or c   Upgrade to the jogging/walking programme.

JOGGING/WALKING PROGRAMME

Jogging is not an ideal aerobic activity because it places the legs and spine under considerable impact and stress. It is not an activity for unfit or elderly people, or for individuals with leg or back injuries. The difference between jogging and running is mainly pace. At anything slower than eight minutes to the mile, you are jogging; any faster and you are running.

The programme below is designed to increase gradually in intensity until you can jog continuously at a moderate pace for twenty minutes or more.

From Stage 2 onwards it can be adapted for running but you should never attempt a running pace unless you have already achieved a high level of fitness. When you are jogging, you should still be able to conduct a conversation. If you cannot, then you should slow down.

You should never jog or run without first warming up, else you substantially increase your risk of strain or injury. The warm-up routine described in chapter 2 will raise your pulse and prepare your body for exercise. Similarly, after you have finished, take your pulse readings and cool down by performing the warm-up exercises in reverse order.

Preliminary Stage
See how long you can jog continuously at a moderate pace, up to a maximum of twenty minutes. If you can do twenty minutes or more, go straight to Stage 3. If you can do twelve minutes, go to Stage 2.

Stage 1
You need to build up your capacity so that you can jog for at least twelve minutes continuously. The best way is through a graduated walking/jogging programme. The table on page 93 shows a sensible rate of progression. Start by jogging for thirty seconds and walking for thirty seconds alternately for a total of twelve minutes. Every four to six times you do this move up a level until you can jog for twelve minutes continuously. At each stage the pattern should be repeated to add up to twelve minutes exercise in total. Then move up to Stage 2.

Always remember to warm up before and cool down after you jog.

Stage 2
Add two minutes to the overall time every four to six times you jog, up to a maximum of twenty minutes. Divide your time in half. Jog out for the first half and back the second half. This helps you keep at a constant speed.

Stage	Time jogging/walking (Repeat pattern for 12 minutes total time)
1	30 seconds jogging, 30 seconds walking
2	1 minute jogging, 1 minute walking
3	1 minute 30 seconds jogging, 1 minute 30 seconds walking
4	2 minutes jogging, 1 minute walking
5	3 minutes jogging, 1 minute walking
6	4 minutes jogging, 1 minute walking
7	5 minutes jogging, 1 minute walking
8	6 minutes jogging, 1 minute walking
9	7 minutes jogging, 1 minute walking
10	8 minutes jogging, 1 minute walking
11	9 minutes jogging, 1 minute walking
12	Jog for 12 minutes

Stage 3

Now you can jog continuously for twenty minutes, you should start to jog faster to build up distance. Always jog for twenty minutes. Do not attempt to do a set distance in a shorter time. Once you have jogged for three consecutive sessions without improvement move up to Stage 4.

Stage 4

You may:

a   Add a further two minutes to the overall time every four to six times you jog, up to a maximum of thirty minutes.

or b Focus on increasing the speed so that you are running instead of jogging.

or c Increase the intensity by jogging up hills or pumping your arms more vigorously which will improve the muscle tone in your body.

or d Vary your speed. For example, try jogging for three minutes at a steady pace and one minute faster.

HINTS ON JOGGING

o   Ensure that you jog in safe and comfortable shoes. Consult a good sports shop if you are in any doubt as to whether your current shoes are suitable. Jogging shoes are worth the expense because they significantly reduce your risk of injury.

o Vary the course which you jog so that your body does not become too accustomed to one particular route.

o Never attempt to jog if you have a bad back or if you have had any recent injuries or operations. If you are in doubt as to whether you should jog, you should consult an exercise specialist or GP first.

FITNESS FOR THE FUTURE

FOCUSING YOUR PROGRAMME ON A SPECIFIC PART OF YOUR BODY

You can personalize your programme to make it focus more specifically on the areas of your body that you most want to work on. Look back at your personal circuit chart in chapter 3. On the right of the table, you will see the letters 'U, B, L and A'.

If you want to work on your upper body (e.g. arms, shoulders, chest), add an extra upper body exercise at the three points marked 'U' on your circuit card by writing in the name of the exercise in the shaded 'U' areas. Duplicate the exercises you currently do or add new upper body exercises from the level below. For example, if you are on upper body Level 2, either duplicate the upper body Level 2 exercises you already do or add the Level 1 upper body exercises.

If you want to work on your back or buttocks, add an extra back exercise at the three points marked 'B' on your circuit card by writing in the name of the exercise in the shaded 'B' areas. Duplicate the exercises you currently do or add new back exercises from the level below. For example, if you are on back Level 2, either duplicate the back Level 2 exercises you already do or add the Level 1 back exercises.

If you want to work on your legs (e.g. calves, thighs), add an extra legs exercise at the three points marked 'L' on your circuit card by writing in the name of the exercise in the shaded 'L' areas. Duplicate the exercises you currently do or add new legs exercises from the level below. For example, if you are on legs Level 2, either duplicate the legs Level 2 exercises you already do or add the Level 1 legs exercises.

PERSONAL CIRCUIT CHART

Specialization ▶

PERSONAL EXERCISE CIRCUIT

Area	Name of exercise	
Legs		UB
Abdominals		L
Back		A
Upper body		
Legs		UB
Abdominals		L
Back		A
Upper body		
Legs		UB
Abdominals		L
Back		A
Upper body		

REPETITIONS

Stage	Repetitions
1	
2	
3	
4	
5	
6	

If you want to work on your abdomen (e.g. stomach, buttocks), add an extra abdomen exercise at the three points marked 'A' on your circuit card by writing in the name of the exercise in the shaded 'A' areas. Duplicate the exercises you currently do or add new exercises from the level below. For example, if you are on abdomen Level 2, either duplicate the abdomen Level 2 exercises you already do or add the Level 1 abdomen exercises.

CHANGING AN EXERCISE

When you are performing a circuit, if you find it too taxing on one particular part of your body, substitute easier exercises. If you find it too easy, substitute harder exercises (Level 1 is the easiest level, Level 3 the hardest). For example, if you found *Half press-ups* too difficult, which is Level 2, you could substitute one of the other upper body Level 2 exercises in your circuit or one of the easier Level 1 exercises such as *Press-ups, all fours*.

The three exercises from each level are approximately at the same level of difficulty, so it is up to you which you choose. Here are some tips to help you:

○ Choose an exercise that does not affect or worsen any injury you may have. Make sure you do not feel pain as you perform the exercise.

○ Choose an exercise that you are sure you understand and feels comfortable.

○ Choose the exercise which feels as if it works the other parts of your body that you are interested in. For example, if you are interested in building up your shoulders and upper body, you should try different exercises and see which works your upper body the most.

CHANGING YOUR PROGRAMME

When you have completed all six stages in your progression level, you will be ready to make your programme harder. Take the fitness test in chapter 2 again. If you have been following the programme consistently, you will see quite an improvement in your scores and by using your new body levels and overall level scores, you can prescribe an entirely new programme for yourself in line with your new abilities.

EXERCISING AFTER A BREAK

If you stop following the programme for any reason such as during sickness or a holiday and you want to start again, fall back one stage of the progression, if the break has been for only a week or so. Fall back to Stage 1 of the progression level if the break has been for more than a week but less than a month. If the break has been for a month or more, take the fitness assessment in chapter 2 again and devise a new programme to start on.

Fitness opportunities

Try to build as much exercise into your daily lifestyle as possible and take advantage of fitness opportunities as they arise:

o   If you travel to work by bus, tube or train, get off one stop earlier and walk the rest of the way at a brisk pace.

o   Avoid car journeys, or bus/tube/train rides that take five minutes or less – walk instead. Walk as often as you can.

o   Use stairs (up and down) wherever possible instead of lifts.

o   Walk to and from the shops carrying the shopping instead of driving. Carry objects instead of using a trolley.

o   After a bath or shower, use a towel vigorously to dry yourself off.

All of these activities, especially walking, increases the rate at which you burn energy during your daily routine, increasing your fitness level and helping you lose fat.

FINAL WORDS

Always remember that the quality of the exercise you do is far more important than the speed or the quantity and that fitness is as much a mental attitude as physical exercise. Train yourself to perform the exercises correctly, carefully and steadily, not to skip levels in order to progress faster and above all, to exercise regularly. Maintaining your motivation is critical to your success.

Get into the 'exercise frame of mind' and remember, what you get out of your Programme will be entirely dependent upon what *you* put into it.

WE WISH YOU WELL AS YOU EXERCISE TOWARDS A FITTER, HEALTHIER AND HAPPIER FUTURE.

THE SUNDAY TIMES
LIFESTYLE FITNESS PROGRAMME

THE VIDEO

LIFESTYLE FITNESS
WITHIN YOUR REACH

17 Minutes -
3 Times A Week

All - Round Fitness
For Men
And Women

REGISTER YOUR PURCHASE

AND JOIN THE **LIFESTYLE ▟FITNESS** CLUB NOW

Return this page to register on the Lifestyle Fitness Programme and join the Lifestyle Fitness Club. In return you will receive:

☆ Hints & tips sheets and details of other Lifestyle Fitness Programmes.

☆ A special telephone number you can use to contact us and receive further information about the Programme.

☆ Advance information about new Lifestyle Fitness books, videos and ˌProgrammes prior to their release.

Please include £1 coin to cover the cost of administration and postage.

Please complete:

Title: Mr / Mrs / Miss / Ms / ....

First Name: ....

Surname: ....

Address: ....

....

.... Postcode: ....

Date of Birth: .... /............ /............

Which Group Are You? (tick one box only)

☐ Director   ☐ Retired

☐ Manager   ☐ Self-Employed

☐ Manual Worker   ☐ Student

☐ Office or Retail Worker   ☐ Housewife

☐ Professional   ☐ Unemployed

☐ Skilled Worker or Tradesman ☐ Other

To register/join, include £1 and send to: Lifestyle Fitness,
Southbank House, Black Prince Road, London SE1 7SJ